The DOG LOVERS' Guides

Bulldog

The DOG LOVERS' Guides

Bulldog

By Beverley Stephenson

Mason Crest
450 Parkway Drive, Suite D
Broomall, PA 19008
www.masoncrest.com

© 2018 by Mason Crest, an imprint of National Highlights, Inc.

Printed and bound in the United States of America.

Series ISBN: 978-1-4222-3848-6
Hardback ISBN: 978-1-4222-3851-6
EBook ISBN: 978-1-4222-7930-4

First printing
1 3 5 7 9 8 6 4 2

Cover photograph by Sunheyy/Dreamstime.com.

Library of Congress Cataloging-in-Publication Data is on file with the publisher.

QR Codes disclaimer:

You may gain access to certain third-party content ("Third-Party Sites") by scanning and using the QR Codes that appear in this publication (the "QR Codes"). We do not operate or control in any respect any information, products, or services on such Third-Party Sites linked to by us via the QR Codes included in this publication, and we assume no responsibility for any materials you may access using the QR Codes. Your use of the QR Codes may be subject to terms, limitations, or restrictions set forth in the applicable terms of use or otherwise established by the owners of the Third-Party Sites. Our linking to such Third-Party Sites via the QR Codes does not imply an endorsement or sponsorship of such Third-Party Sites, or the information, products, or services offered on or through the Third-Party Sites, nor does it imply an endorsement or sponsorship of this publication by the owners of such Third-Party Sites.

Contents

Key Icons to Look For

 Sidebars: This boxed material within the main text allows readers to build knowledge, gain insights, explore possibilities, and broaden their perspectives by weaving together additional information to provide realistic and holistic perspectives.

 Educational Videos: Readers can view videos by scanning our QR codes, providing them with additional educational content to supplement the text. Examples include news coverage, moments in history, speeches, iconic moments, and much more!

 Series Glossary of Key Terms: This back-of-the-book glossary contains terminology used throughout this series. Words found here increase the reader's ability to read and comprehend higher-level books and articles in this field.

Chapter 1

Introducing the Bulldog

The Bulldog may be the ugly mug of the dog world, but there is probably no other breed that has such a devoted fan club. He has evolved from his days as a fearless bull baiter to become the most loyal and affectionate of companions.

There are many different variations on the type of dog known as a Bulldog or a Bully breed. The breed described in this book is also called the English Bulldog or the British Bulldog.

Physical characteristics

There is no mistaking the Bulldog for any other breed. He is truly unique and it is a case of once seen, never forgotten. Strong and muscular, the Bulldog is short, broad, powerful, and compact. His back rises from the shoulders and then curves down toward a short tail that may be straight or screwed. The Bulldog moves with a characteristic, rolling gait—another breed specialty.

His head is his outstanding feature, with his short muzzle, flattened nose, undershot jaw, and heavy, overhanging flews (lips). His dark, round eyes have a stoic expression, but also one that says, "Don't mess with me."

He has a smooth, short coat that comes in a variety of colors and patterns.

What is a brachycephalic breed?

Brachycephalic breeds that have a foreshortened muzzle and a flattened nose. Other brachycephalic breeds include the Pug, Boxer, French Bulldog, Shih Tzu, and Pekingese.

This type of head construction looks highly distinctive but it should never be exaggerated, because too flat a face can have an adverse effect on a dog's health and well-being. The short muzzle and pushed-back nose can lead to difficulties with breathing. The superficial sign of this is the snores your Bulldog will undoubtedly do. But on a more serious note, he may suffer from labored breathing, particularly in hot weather.

Temperament

The Bulldog began as a fighting dog, but he has left this legacy far behind and is now regarded as one of the most outstanding companion dogs. The breed standard, which is a written blueprint for the breed, says, "The disposition should be equable and kind, resolute and courageous (not vicious or aggressive), and demeanor should be pacific and dignified."

He has a complex character: He's tough, gritty, determined, and loyal, but also has a wicked sense of humor, and seems to delight in playing the clown. The Bulldog looks like a mini tank, but inside that tough exterior is a sweet-natured dog who is lavish with his gifts of love and affection. The Bulldog is alert, and takes a lively interest in everything going on, but there are times when he is sleeping (and snoring . . .) that he is clearly saying, "Do not disturb!"

He's bold. This dates back to the Bulldog's history as a bull baiter, and to this day he shows great confidence and self-assurance. Loyalty is also an integral part of the Bulldog's character, and is the prime reason why he is so highly valued as a companion dog.

He's a dependable, reliable dog with a sound temperament and can be trusted in all situations. And he is courageous—again, a throwback to his days as a bull fighter. This quality is rarely tested, but most Bulldogs have a quiet confidence and will give a good account of themselves if challenged.

Fierce in appearance but possessed of an affectionate nature: What a delightful combination!

Living with a Bulldog

The Bulldog is an adaptable dog and will fit in with most family situations. He adores children, but because he is not a high-energy dog, he can also be an entertaining companion for older people.

He is equally happy in the town or in the country, and will scarcely notice whether you have a mansion or a small apartment—with the proviso that he doesn't have to climb stairs.

The Bulldog is not the most energetic of breeds. Adolescent dogs may go through an excitable period, but most adults will be content with moderate exercise, which means they can fit in with many different lifestyles. One word of warning: The male is bigger and stronger than the female, and he can be a bit of a handful while he is growing up. This means that a Bulldog—particularly a male Bulldog—may not be the best choice for anyone who is frail or infirm.

That said, the Bulldog has so few drawbacks as a breed, it is little wonder that he is growing in popularity. After all, who can resist the unique charm of a dog who looks like a battle-axe on the outside, but is kind and gentle on the inside?

Tracing back in time

This most amiable of animals has come a long way from his days as a fierce guard and courageous bull baiter. But throughout his long history there is a common thread—the Bulldog has always been highly valued by his human companions for his steadfast loyalty.

The ancient ancestors of Bulldogs may trace back as far as ancient times. Roman writers described fierce Greek Molosser dogs. Molosser dogs are the ancestors of today's Mastiffs and Bulldogs.

It is thought that Phoenician traders introduced these Molossian hounds to Britain around 600 BCE. They were used for their hunting skills, but also found a role as war dogs and guard dogs. Strabo, a contemporary of Julius Caesar, wrote in his description of Britain in 64-63 BCE, "It produces corn, cattle, gold, silver and iron, which also forms its exports together with skins, slaves, and dogs of a superior breed for the chase. The Gauls use these dogs in war, as well as others of their own breed." The Romans called these British fighting dogs *pugnance britannicii,* and imported many of the dogs from Britain. They had strong, compact bodies and short faces—features which are recognizable in today's Bulldog.

Bull baiting

While the origins of the Bulldog are shrouded in antiquity, historians do agree that the name comes from the fact that these dogs were used to control and bait bulls. It was once believed that baiting a bull before slaughter improved the meat, so butchers kept these dogs.

Bull baiting eventually became a popular sport, as well, and a variety of Molosser-type dogs were bred for this purpose. But soon fans realized that a smaller dog who could fly at the bull's head and grab his nose, or any part of his face, in his powerful jaws could bring a bull down and pin it. Eventually, there were bull rings in all the major market towns in Britain. Big crowds came to view the spectacle and gambling was fierce. The Bulldog's courage was legendary.

In 1631, an Englishman named Prestwich Eaton, who was living in Spain, sent a letter to a friend in London asking him to send "A good Mastive dog, a case of liquor, and I beg you to get for me some good bulldoggs." It's the first written record we have that the smaller Bulldog was becoming distinct from the larger Mastiff.

In 1872, a British breeder and exhibitor writing under the name Idstone published a book titled *The Dog, with Simple Directions for His Treatment*, describing what he called the best dogs of the day. By then bull baiting was illegal, but he described what it had been like. He observed that although Bulldogs were small and low, when once they seized the bull's throat "you might sooner cut them in pieces than make them let go their hold." However, the sport of bull baiting came at a price. Many dogs were killed, "The bull tossing them up in the air like footballs."

End of an Era

In 1835, the Humane Act of Parliament abolished public baiting of bulls and bears, and dog fighting. This signaled the end of the bull ring as a place of entertainment. Unfortunately, it was replaced by an undercover world of dog fighting. The dog pit required a smaller, faster, more agile dog, so Bulldogs were interbred with terriers to produce the Bull Terrier and the Staffordshire Bull Terrier.

The Bulldog was no longer needed to bait bulls. But enthusiasts were determined that this loyal, affectionate, and distinctly British dog should not be lost.

Developing the breed

A new sport—dog showing—was emerging, with the first official show staged in Britain in 1859. The following year, the Birmingham show offered classes for Bulldogs, and so there was a new incentive to keep the breed alive. In 1864 the first Bulldog Club was formed, with 30 members. It lasted only three years, but that was long enough to write the first breed standard.

In 1875, the Bulldog Club that still exists today in Britain was founded at the Blue Post Inn in London. It predates the Kennel Club, and has the distinction of being the oldest breed club in the world. Its main objective was to control the influx of Spanish Bulldogs, which were much larger, and to create a breed standard for a moderate size dog.

The club held an annual show for Bulldogs in London, and also licensed shows in other cities. It issues a list of club judges, who were elected annually.

The first Champions

The breed's first champion was Old King Dick, owned by Jacob Lamphier of Sheffield. He was a red smut dog (a reddish brown base color with a black overlay), weighing 48 pounds (22 kg). He won his title at the Birmingham show in 1865 and was a universal favorite with judges throughout his illustrious career. Another of Lamphier's

dogs, Adam, was the first Bulldog entered in the Kennel Club Stud Book.

Sadly, Old Dick's career was cut short in heartbreaking circumstances, which sum up the Bulldog's character. Lamphier, contracted tuberculosis and for the last 12 months of his life he was confined to his room, with Old King Dick as his constant companion. When Jacob died, Old King Dick was distraught, searching for him from room to room, and eventually lying down on a rug in front of the fire in sad resignation. He never lifted his head again; he refused all food and died four days later.

Ch. Old King Dick's memory lived on in his progeny, many of whom proved to be top-quality show dogs. His most influential descendant was a dog called Crib, also known as Sheffield Crib, or Turton's Crib, who was bred by Jacob Lamphier's son.

Crib was a brindle and white dog, weighing a hefty 64 pounds (29 kg). He was born in 1871 and was never beaten in the show ring. At the Bulldog Club shows in 1892 and 1893, he figured in the pedigree of every Bulldog entered.

Bulldogs in the USA

British settlers to the New World took their dogs with them, and this included the Bulldog. The first record is of a dog called Donald, a brindle and White Bulldog sent over by Irish exhibitor, Sir William Verner, to take part in the 1880 New York show. Other early show dogs included Noble and Bonnie Boy. The Bulldog was officially recognized by the American Kennel Club in 1886.

The Bulldog Club of America was founded in 1890 by H.D. Kendall of Lowell, Massachusetts. Its first members were a group of men in the Northeast who wanted to encourage the "thoughtful and careful breeding of the English Bulldog in America."

The best Bulldogs at the time were being shown by Colonel John E. Thayer, the first president of the Bulldog Club of America. He was passionate about the breed and he brought significant imports from Britain, including the dog Robinson Crusoe and the bitch Ch. Britomartis.

In 1921, the first Bulldog was featured on a Mack truck, and in 1922, the Marine Corps took on the Bulldog as its mascot. A number of universities soon did the same, including Georgia, Yale, Butler, and Georgetown. According to AKC registration statistics, the Bulldog was the fifth-most popular dog in America between 1910 and 1920. (By 1973 it had fallen to number 41, but it shot to number six in 2010, and to number four today.)

The current scene

As with many breeds, the Bulldog's popularity has not really been a benefit. With its large head, flat face, heavy body, and somewhat short legs, it's all to easy to breed dogs with exaggerated features or who are structurally unsound. Unscrupulous breeders who are more interested in quantity than quality have produced dogs who, while still loving companions, spend too much time at the veterinarian dealing with breathing problems and joint problems.

This is why it is so very important to get your Bulldog from a reputable breeder who cares deeply about the breed and has invested the time and money to screen their breeding dogs for health problems.

Chapter 2

What Should a Bulldog Look Like?

The Bulldog, with her thick set, low-slung body, and massive short-faced head has attracted a worldwide fan club. What makes a Bulldog so special?

Every pedigreed breed has a breed standard, which is a written blueprint describing how a dog should look, how she should move, and what her temperament should be like. At a dog show, the judge compares all dogs to the standard. The one who most closely embodies the ideal takes home the blue ribbon.

The breed standard has significance beyond the sport of showing, though, because the dogs who win in the ring will be used for breeding. The winners of today are therefore responsible for passing on their genes to future generations and preserving the breed in its best form.

This has major significance today, when breeders are being encouraged to produce Bulldogs without exaggeration, putting health

and the ability to function above the dictates of fashion. The aim is to produce a typical Bulldog, with all the charm that is so strongly associated with the breed, but avoiding the pitfalls of breeding dogs who are adversely affected by their conformation.

General appearance

The Bulldog is a powerfully built, compact dog who is somewhat low in stature. She has a heavy, thick-set body, massive head, wide shoulders, and sturdy limbs. The standard says her general appearance and attitude "should suggest great stability, vigor, and strength."

Her short-faced head is large in proportion to her body, but not

so much as to destroy the general symmetry. She should convey an impression of determination, strength, and activity. She has a broad, short muzzle, but this should not interfere with her breathing.

Females are not so grand or well-developed as males. In fact, the standard says, "In comparison of specimens of different sex, due allowance should be made in favor of the bitches, which do not bear the characteristics of the breed to the same degree of perfection and grandeur as do the dog."

A mature male weighs around 50 pounds (23 kg) and a female is about 40 pounds (18 kg).

Head and skull

The Bulldog head is the outstanding characteristic of the breed, and the standard gives a very detailed description of what the perfect Bulldog head should look like.

The skull is relatively large in circumference and measures at least the same as the height of the dog at the shoulders. The forehead is flat, with finely wrinkled skin; the cheeks are well developed, extending sideways beyond the eyes.

The stop, the step-up between the muzzle and the forehead, is defined; the face from the front of the cheekbone to the nose is relatively short and may be slightly wrinkled. The muzzle is short and broad, turning upward.

The nose and the nostrils are large, broad, and black. A dog with a brown or liver-colored nose is disqualified in the show ring. The Bulldog may have a nose-roll, a fold of skin above the nose, and this may be full or split.

The flews are thick, broad, and deep, covering the lower jaw at both sides. The teeth should not be visible when the dog's mouth is closed.

Eyes

When looking at a Bulldog head-on, the eyes are low down the skull, well away from the ears. They are positioned wide apart and should be in a straight line with the stop. They are round, and should be neither prominent nor sunken. When looking forward, no white of the eye should be visible. You also should not be able to see the haw—the third eyelid—in the lower corner of the eye. The eyes should be very dark—almost black.

Ears

The ears are set high, almost as if they were on the top corners of the skull. They are placed wide apart and as far from the eyes as possible. Small and thin, the rose-shaped ears fold backward to display part of the inside of the ear.

Mouth

The jaws are broad and square, and the bite is undershot, with the lower jaw projecting in front of the upper jaw. The teeth are large and strong, with the canine teeth (the fangs) set well apart and the six small teeth between the canines set in an even, level row.

Forequarters

The shoulders are broad, sloping, and deep. They are very muscular and powerful and give the impression of being tacked onto the body. The elbows are low and stand well out from the body. The chest is wide, prominent, and deep.

Neck

The neck is moderate in length, thick, deep, and strong. It should be well-arched at the back with some loose skin around the throat, forming a dewlap (a loose, fold of skin) on either side.

Body

The back is short and strong, broad at the shoulders and comparatively narrow at the loins.

A breed characteristic is a roach back; this is seen as a fall in the topline behind the shoulders, rising to the loins (which are higher than the shoulders) and curving more suddenly to the tail, forming a slight arch. The rib cage is well-rounded and deep, giving the dog a broad, short-legged appearance.

Hindquarters

The back legs are large and muscular and are slightly longer than the front legs. The stifles (knees) turn very slightly away from the body; the hocks (ankles) are slightly bent.

Feet

The feet are compact and moderate in size. The toes are well split, with high knuckles and short, stubby nails.

Tail

The tail may be either straight or screwed, but never curved or curly. Either way, it should be short, with a thick root and narrower tip. It must be hung low and carried downward. A high tail set is considered a fault, as this would result in the tail being carried above the line of the back.

A straight tail should be cylindrical and of uniform taper. A screwed tail should have well-defined kinks, but all should be carried below the base or root.

Movement

The Bulldog has a unique way of moving, with short, quick steps on the tips of her toes. The back feet appear to skim the ground. The standard says, "The style and carriage are peculiar, his gait being a loose-jointed, shuffling, sidewise motion, giving the characteristic 'roll.' The action must, however, be unrestrained, free and vigorous."

It is the peculiar conformation of the Bulldog—her wide-set front legs, narrow loin, and longer rear legs—that produce the characteristic rolling gait. Good conformation results in sound movement; poor conformation will inevitably produce poor movement.

Summing Up

Although the majority of Bulldogs are kept as pet dogs and will never be exhibited in the show ring, it is important that breeders strive for perfection and try to produce dogs who conform as closely as possible to the breed standard.

Coat and Color

The coat should be straight, short, flat, close to the body, smooth, and glossy. It should have a fine texture, with no fringe, feathering, or curling.

The pure, brilliant color is a feature of the breed. Solid colors are red, white, fawn, fallow (blond), or any combination of those colors. Patterns and markings include brindle (brown or red with darker streaks), piebald (a white dog with colored patches), ticking (colored spots in the white parts of the coat), black masks, black tipping, and a minimal amount of solid black in piebalds. White dogs sometimes have black freckles. The colored patches in piebalds might be brindle or ticked.

This has become particularly important with the Bulldog, where exaggeration has led to very real health issues. Breeders need to retain all that is unique in this very special breed, but the top priority must be to produce typical examples of the breed who are sound in mind and body.

Indeed, the standard calls for overall symmetry, and cautions, "The 'points' should be well-distributed and bear good relation one to the other, no feature being in such prominence from either excess or lack of quality that the animal appears deformed or ill-proportioned."

Chapter 3

What Do You Want From Your Bulldog?

There are more than 200 dog breeds to choose from, so how can you be sure the Bulldog is the right breed for you? Before you take the plunge into Bulldog ownership, you need to be 100 percent sure that this breed best suits your lifestyle.

Companion

The Bulldog's raison d'être is to be with people, and he is the perfect family companion. He is intensely loyal, and cares deeply about all members of his family. He may be more respectful of the grown-ups, but children are of equal importance to him. He is loving and affectionate—and also very tolerant. If he's raised responsibly, once he is mature this laid-back canine tends to take life as it comes.

These qualities are perfect for many different types of owners. But if you are highly energetic and want a long-distance walking companion—or a running companion at any distance—you will need to think again. A fit Bulldog will enjoy some exercise, but nothing overrides his love of creature comforts. Lazing around at home, surrounded by his loved ones, is his top priority, so make sure you share his outlook on life.

Sports dog

There are lots of canine sports to choose from, but if this is an area that interests you, the Bulldog may not be the breed for you.

His overall physical conformation does not lend itself to demanding or speedy sports. He is certainly clever, but he is not highly

motivated to perform tasks without good reason.

However, with positive, consistent training, you will make head-way in the sports he can do. And even though your Bulldog may not be a record-setter, you will be interacting with him and spending quality time with him, which will enhance your relationship.

Show dog

Do you have ambitions to exhibit your Bulldog in the show ring? This is a highly competitive sport, with large entries at the big dog shows, so you do need the right dog to begin with.

If you plan to show your Bulldog, you will have to track down a show quality puppy, and train him to perform in the show ring. He has to learn how to show himself off to advantage and accept the hands-on examination that he will be subjected to when being judged.

It is also important to bear in mind that not every puppy with show potential develops into a top-quality dog. You must, therefore, be prepared to love your Bulldog and give him a home for life, even if he doesn't make the grade as a show dog.

What does your Bulldog want from you?

A dog cannot speak for himself, so we need to view the world from a canine perspective and figure out what a Bulldog needs to live a happy, contented, and fulfilling life.

Time and commitment

A Bulldog needs a commitment that you will care for him for his en-tire life—guiding him through his puppyhood, enjoying his adulthood, and being there for him in his later years. If all dog owners were prepared to make this commitment, there would be hardly any dogs in shelters and rescue groups.

The Bulldog's place is in the heart of the family, and he will be thoroughly miserable if he is excluded from family activities or has to spend long periods of time on his own. A dog should not be left for longer than four hours at a stretch; if you cannot fulfill this obligation, you would be wise to delay taking on a dog of any breed until your situation changes.

Practical matters

Practically speaking, the Bulldog is a relatively easy breed to care for. He needs minimal grooming (aside from a daily face wash to keep those wrinkle folds healthy), and once you have found a diet that suits him, there should be no problems with feeding him.

The laid-back Bulldog will not demand to be taken out, and some can be positively lazy. However, it is your responsibility to keep your

Bulldog fit and healthy. A routine of varied exercise will be good for him physically, and it will also provide mental stimulation as he investigates the world around him.

Consistent expectations

The Bulldog is a loyal and affectionate dog and rarely feels the need to be pushy. However, he is also a big dog, so it's important that everyone in the family—big and small—feels confident that the dog will cooperate with them. This is all about building a relationship based on trust, and it starts from the moment your Bulldog arrives in your home. You are the provider of good things—food and shelter, care and exercise, play and love. In addition, you set the boundaries, and as long as you are clear and consistent about them, so your Bulldog understands what is expected of him, he will be content to comply with your requests.

If you fail to clearly and consistently communicate what you want, your Bulldog will have no option but to invent his own agenda, and will be confused if you try to impose your will. The secret is to start as you mean to go on: Be a kind, caring, and consistent dog owner and you will be rewarded with a companion who is second to none.

Other considerations

Now that you have decided a Bulldog is perfect for your family, you can narrow your choice so you know exactly what you are looking for.

Male or female?

Whether you choose a male or a female is a matter of personal preference. Bulldogs are very much individuals, so there are no hard and fast rules about temperament differences between the genders. However, there are a few generalizations that are worth noting.

The male is physically bigger and stronger than the female, and he has more presence. He can be headstrong, particularly when

young and adolescent, but with guidance, he will mature into a loyal and loving companion.

A female Bulldog cares deeply about her home and family, and she can be protective. This is okay in moderation, but it is not behavior that should be encouraged. Female Bulldogs do not always get along well together, and if there is a falling out—even between a mother and daughter—it can result in ongoing problems. This is worth considering if you are adding to your Bulldog family.

If you choose a female, you will need to cope with her heat seasons, which will start at around eight months of age and occur approximately every nine months thereafter. During the three-week period of a season, you will need to keep your bitch away from males who have not been neutered to eliminate the risk of an unwanted pregnancy. Some owners report that females may be a little moody and withdrawn during their seasonal cycle. Many pet owners decide to spay their girls, which puts an end to the seasons and also has some health benefits. The operation is usually done when the dog is about six months old. The best plan is to seek advice from your veterinarian.

An unneutered male may not cause many problems, although some do have a stronger tendency to urine mark, including inside the house. However, training will usually put a stop to this. An unneutered male will also be on the lookout for bitches in season, and this may lead to difficulties, depending on your circumstances. Neutering (castrating) a male is a relatively simple operation, and there are associated health benefits. Again, you should seek advice from your veterinarian.

Color?

The Bulldog comes in a variety of colors, ranging from white through a range of fawns to red. In terms of markings, Bulldogs may be brindled or piebald or have a mask or ticking. If you are

Choosing a rescued dog

It is rare to find a Bulldog in a shelter or an all-breed rescue group. However, many breed clubs run their own rescue groups, and this is where you will find dogs who were given up from their first homes. (You'll find the Bulldog Rescue Network at www.rescue bulldogs.org.)

Sometimes a dog needs to be rehomed through no fault of his own, usually when a family's circumstances change. The reasons range from illness or death to family breakdown, changing jobs, or even the arrival of a new baby.

Occasionally, a Bulldog may not have received the all-important training that every dog needs, and he may have become too much for his family to cope with. This is unusual, because Bulldogs are generally easy to live with. But it could be that an individual, left to his own devices, has become too headstrong, or he may have developed anxieties if he has not been properly socialized.

If you decide you want to adopt a rescued Bulldog, try to find out as much as you can about the dog's history, so you know exactly what you are taking on. You need to be aware of his age and health status, his likes and dislikes, plus any behavioral issues that may be relevant. You need to be realistic about what you are capable of achieving, so you can be sure you can give the dog a permanent home.

Regardless of the dog's history, he'll need plenty of time and patience as he settles into his new home. It may take weeks, or even months before he becomes fully part of the family. But if all goes well, you will have the reward of knowing that you have given a Bulldog a second chance.

exhibiting your Bulldog in the show ring, you will be looking for more symmetrical markings. In the U.S., the merle pattern (a solid color that's broken up with irregular patches of two other colors) is a disqualification in the show ring. But for the pet owner, color is purely a matter of personal preference. It's much better to choose your dog based on temperament and health.

English Bulldog breed basics

More than one?

Bulldogs can be addictive, and you may decide two dogs would suit your lifestyle and would be company for each other. Again, females do not always get along well together, so bear this in mind if you are adding to your Bulldog population.

Regardless of what sex you choose, do not get two puppies from the same litter, or even two of a similar age. The two puppies will have no problem with the plan; they will always have a dog to play with. But this could be at the cost of forming a strong bond with members of their human family.

You also need to consider the effect that rearing two puppies will have on your life. Looking after one puppy is hard work, but taking on two pups at the same time is more than double the workload. Housetraining is a nightmare. Often you don't even know which puppy is having lapses, and training is impossible unless you separate the two puppies and give them one-on-one attention.

Be very wary of a breeder who encourages you to buy two puppies from the same litter, as it is unlikely the welfare of the puppies is their top priority. Most responsible breeders have a waiting list of potential puppy buyers before a litter is even born, and have no need to make this type of sale.

If you do decide to add to your Bulldog population, wait at least 18 months, until your first dog is fully trained and settled, before taking on another puppy.

An adult dog

You may decide to miss out on the puppy phase and take on an adult dog instead. Such a dog may be harder to find, but sometimes a breeder will rehome a female when her breeding career is at an end, so she can enjoy the benefits of getting more individual attention. In some cases, the breeder may have kept a dog a show and/or breeding prospect, and then found the dog did not turn out as expected but will still make an excellent pet.

There are advantages to taking on an adult dog, because you know exactly what you are getting. But the upheaval of changing homes can be quite upsetting, so you will need to have plenty of patience during the settling-in period.

Chapter 4

Finding Your Puppy

Your aim is to find a healthy puppy who is typical of the breed, is physically sound, and has been reared with the greatest possible care. Where to start?

One great way to find your puppy is to attend a dog show. This will give you the opportunity to see a wide range of Bulldogs of different colors and different ages. If you look closely, you will also see different physical types—maybe some small variations in head size or body type or length of face. They are all purebred Bulldogs, but breeders produce dogs with a family likeness, so you can see which type you prefer.

When the judging is finished, talk to the exhibitors and find out more about their dogs. They may not have puppies available, but most will be planning a litter, and you may decide to put your name on a waiting list.

Bear in mind that breeding Bulldogs can be difficult. Because of the large head, there is a higher incidence of cesarean births than

in other breeds. For this reason, breeders limit the number of litters they produce, which often means lengthy waiting lists. This can be frustrating, but if you have decided that a Bulldog is the breed for you, you must be patient—it will be worth the wait!

Internet research

The Internet is an excellent resource, but when it comes to finding a puppy, use it with care.

Do go to the websites of the American Kennel Club (AKC) and the United Kennel Club (UKC). Both have excellent websites that will give you information about the Bulldog as a breed, and advice about what to look for when choosing a puppy. The AKC site will have some links to breeders who have puppies available; look for

breeders of merit, who adhere to an AKC code of conduct.

Do go to the websites of the Bulldog Club of America and local Bulldog breed clubs. You will find lots of useful information that will help you to care for your Bulldog. There may be contact details of breeders in your

Bulldog puppies at play

area, or you may need to go through the club secretary. Some websites also have a list of breeders who have puppies available. The advantage of going through a breed club is that members will follow a code of ethics, and this will give you some guarantees regarding breeding practices and health checks.

If you are planning to show your Bulldog you will obviously want to go to a breeder who has had some success in the ring. You will need to do additional research to discover more about their breeding lines and the type of Bulldog they produce.

Do not look at puppies for sale on the Internet. There are legitimate Bulldog breeders with their own websites, and they may, occasionally, advertise a litter, although in most cases reputable breeders have waiting lists for their puppies.

The danger comes from unscrupulous breeders who produce puppies purely for profit, with no thought for the health of the dogs they breed and no care given to rearing the litter. Photos of puppies are hard to resist, but never make a decision based purely on an advertisement. You need to find out who the breeder is, and have the opportunity to visit their premises and inspect the litter (and their mother) before making a decision.

Questions, questions, questions

When you find a breeder with puppies available, you will have lots of questions to ask. These should include:

- Where have the puppies been reared? Hopefully, they will be in a home environment, which gives them the best possible start in life.
- What health checks have the parents had?
- How many are in the litter? What is the split of males and females? What colors are available?
- How many have already been spoken for? (The breeder will almost certainly be keeping a puppy to show or for breeding, and there may well be others on a waiting list.)
- Can I see the mother with her puppies?
- What age are the puppies?

- When will they be ready to go to their new homes?

Bear in mind that puppies need to be with their mother and siblings until they are 10 to 12 weeks of age; otherwise they miss out on vital learning and communication skills, which will have a detrimental effect on them for the rest of their lives.

You should also be prepared to answer a number of questions from the breeder. They will want to make sure you are suitable as a potential owner of one of their precious puppies. You will be asked some or all of the following questions:

- How big is your home?
- Do you have a fenced backyard?
- Do you have children/grandchildren? What are their ages?
- Is there somebody at home the majority of the time?
- What is your previous experience with dogs?
- Do you have plans to show your Bulldog?

The breeder is not being intrusive, so please don't be offended. They need to understand the type of home you will be able to provide, so they can to make the right match. This is for both the dog's benefit and yours.

Steer clear of a breeder who does not ask you questions. He or she may be more interested in making money from the puppies than ensuring they go to good homes. They may also have taken other shortcuts that may prove disastrous, and very expensive, in terms of vet bills and heartache.

Health issues

As with all purebred dogs, the Bulldog suffers from some hereditary health problems. Many of these have tests to detect them, so breeders can avoid breeding carriers or structurally unsound dogs. You need to talk to the breeder about the health status of breeding stock and find out if there are any issues or concerns. (Chapter 9 has more information about hereditary health issues in Bulldogs.)

Puppy watching

Bulldog puppies are totally irresistible, and when you see a litter you will want to take them all home with you! However, you must try to put your feelings aside so that you can make an informed choice. You need to be 100 percent confident that the parents are healthy, and the puppies have been reared with love and care, before making a commitment to buy.

Looking at a litter

It is a good idea to have a mental checklist of what to look out for when you visit a breeder.

You want to see:

- A clean, healthy environment with no foul odors or messes.
- Puppies who are outgoing, friendly, and eager to meet you. You do not want to see any fear, shyness, or aggression.
- Lively pups who are keen to play.
- A sweet-natured mother who is ready to show off her babies.
- Puppies who are well-fleshed out but not pot-bellied, which could be an indication of worms.
- Bright eyes, with no sign of soreness or discharge.
- Clean ears that smell fresh.
- No discharge from the nose.
- Clean rear ends—matting could indicate upset tummies.

It is important that you see the mother with her puppies, as this will give you a good idea of the temperament they are likely to inherit. It is also helpful if you can see other close relatives, so you can see the type of Bulldogs the breeder produces.

In most cases, you will not be able to see the father (sire), because most breeders will travel some distance to find a stud dog who is not too close to their own bloodlines and who complements the characteristics of their bitch. However, you should be able to see photos of him and have a chance to examine his pedigree and show record.

Companion puppy

If you are looking for a Bulldog purely as a companion, you should be guided by the breeder, who will have spent hours and hours puppy watching, and will know each of the pups as individuals. It is tempting to choose a puppy yourself, but the breeder will take into account your family and lifestyle, and will help you to pick the most suitable puppy.

Show puppy

If you are buying a puppy with the hope of showing her, make sure you make this clear to the breeder. A lot of planning goes into a litter, and although all the puppies will have been reared with equal care, there will be only one or two who have show potential.

Ideally, recruit a breed expert to look at the puppies with you, so you have the benefit of their objective evaluation. The breeder will also be there to help, as they will want to ensure that only the best puppies from their kennel are exhibited in the show ring. The optimum age to select a show puppy is between seven and eight weeks, when she will look like a miniature version of the adult dog. Thereafter, she will go through different phases and may look different from one week to the next, before she reaches full maturity.

A puppy with show potential should have a stocky, short-backed body. As chapter 2 explained, a roach back, where the rear end is higher that the shoulders, is a feature of the breed. This should be evident in a puppy, but not exaggerated. She should have a well-defined neck and good front and rear angulation.

Within a litter there will be a variety of straight and screwed tails; the length and shape of tail will also vary. Both are equally acceptable in the show ring. When looking at a puppy with a straight tail, look for a low set, with the tail carried downward. Certainly, a tightly screwed tail should be avoided on health grounds.

The Bulldog's head is of paramount importance in show dogs, and an expert will be able to assess specific features to judge whether a puppy has the potential to meet the exacting description in the breed standard. You will be looking for:

- A brick-shaped head when viewed from the front and the side.
- The top of the skull should be flat and broad. There should be some wrinkling but it should not be excessive.
- At eight weeks the ears will probably hang forward, but if they are small and thin, they should develop into the ideal rose shape by the time a puppy is around four months of age.
- The nose and nostrils should be large and black.
- The eyes should be round, dark, set wide apart, and on the same straight line as the stop (the step up between the muzzle and the forehead).
- When you look at the puppy's mouth from straight on, the front lower jaw should be directly beneath the upper jaw.

Remember, temperament and health should always be major considerations. The time you spend showing a dog during her lifetime is very small compared to the time spent living at home as a treasured member of your family.

Chapter 5

A Bulldog-Friendly Home

I t may seem like forever until your Bulldog puppy is ready to leave the breeder and move to his new home. You can fill the time by getting your house and yard ready, and buying all the supplies you will need. These preparations are for a new puppy, but actually, they are the way you will create an environment that is safe and secure for your Bulldog throughout his life.

In the home

Nothing is safe when a puppy is around, and the Bulldog is certainly no exception. Everything is new and exciting for a young puppy—and it all needs a thorough investigation!

Bulldog puppies are generally less hyper than some of the working breeds, but without a doubt, a free-ranging Bulldog puppy cannot be trusted. Remember, it is not only your prized possessions that are under threat; a puppy can inflict just as much damage on himself.

Electric cords and cables are a major hazard, so these will need to be secured out of reach. You will need to make sure all cabinets and storage units cannot be opened—or broken into. This applies particularly in the kitchen and bathroom, where you may store cleaning materials and other substances that could be toxic to dogs.

There are a number of household plants that are poisonous, so these will need to relocated, along with anything at all that is breakable.

A Bulldog puppy is heavy relative to his size, which means while he is growing, his joints are vulnerable and any mishap could prove serious. Puppies bounding up and down the stairs are not a good idea, so many owners find it easier to keep their puppy on the main floor of their home right from the start. The best way of doing this is to use a baby gate; these can also be useful if you want to limit your Bulldog's freedom in any other part of the house.

In the yard

The Bulldog is very much a people dog and he has no plans to escape from the comforts of his home and the companionship of his beloved family. However, it is essential that your yard is fenced to a minimum height of 4 feet (1.2 meters), and gates must close and latch securely. A Bulldog puppy loves to explore and will squeeze himself out of a gap in the fence, just to see what is on the other side!

He may also take an interest in gardening, which may involve some concentrated digging or possibly sampling some of your plants. This can be very annoying, especially if you are proud of your garden, but, worse still, it can be positively dangerous.

There are a number of plants that are toxic to dogs, and the consequence of ingesting poisonous plants could be very serious. You therefore need to find out which plants might be poisonous and take preventive action before your puppy arrives in his new home.

Find out if your garden contains plants that are poisonous to dogs. (There is not enough room to list them all here, but you can find a full list at www.aspca.org/pet-care/animal-poison-control/toxic-and-non-toxic-plants.) You might decide to fence off part of your garden, to make sure the yard is absolutely Bulldog-friendly.

Swimming pools and ponds should be covered. Most puppies are fearless, and although it is easy for a puppy to take the plunge, it is virtually impossible for him to get out—with potentially lethal consequences.

You will also need to designate a toileting area in the yard. This will help with the housetraining process, and it will also make cleaning up easier.

Remember, Bulldogs are valuable animals, so you need to guard against the possibility of intruders getting into your yard, as well. You must be always careful about leaving your Bulldog (puppy or adult) unattended in the yard or tied up outside a shop or restaurant.

House rules

Before your puppy comes home, hold a family conference to decide on the house rules. You need to decide which rooms your puppy will have access to, and establish whether he is to be allowed on the furniture or not. It is important to start as you mean to go on. You cannot invite a puppy onto the sofa for cuddles, only to decide in a few months' time that he's no longer allowed up.

The Bulldog likes to please, but he can sometimes follow his own agenda and be a little stubborn if he you try to change things he has already learned. However, if house rules are applied consistently right from the start, he will understand what is—and what is not—allowed, and he will soon learn to cooperate.

It's a simple rule: No matter how cute, don't allow your puppy to do anything you don't want him to do as an adult.

Going shopping

There are some essential items you will need for your Bulldog. It's best to get everything before your dog comes home, so you'll be all ready for him. If you choose wisely, much of it will last for many years to come.

Indoor crate

Raising a puppy is so much easier if you invest in an indoor crate. It provides a safe haven for your puppy at night, when you have to go out during the day, and at other times when you

Puppy crate training

cannot supervise him. A puppy needs a base where he feels safe and secure, and where he can rest undisturbed. An indoor crate provides the perfect den, and many adult dogs continue to use them throughout their lives. Bearing this in mind, it is sensible to buy a crate that will be big enough for your Bulldog when he is fully grown. The recommended size is 30-by-20-by-24 inches (76-by-51-by-61 cm).

What starts as a safe place for keeping your puppy when you cannot supervise him soon becomes your dog's favorite resting place. If you leave the crate door open, you will find that your adult Bulldog will choose to go in and out of his crate.

You will also need to consider where you are going to put the crate. The kitchen is usually the most suitable place, as this is the hub of family life. Try to find a snug corner where the puppy can rest when he wants to, but where he can also see what is going on around him, and still be with the family.

Exercise pen

These are becoming increasingly popular with Bulldog owners. They provide a more spacious alternative to a crate, and can be used indoors or out. The puppy has room in his pen to play, but is still safely confined.

A puppy should not be left in an exercise pen if you are going out or if you are elsewhere in the house for an extended period of time. However, it provides a safe option when you are busy—cleaning the house, for example—and do not want your puppy to get involved. An exercise pen has the added benefit that it has good visibility, so your pup does not feel excluded from the family's activities.

Beds and bedding

The crate should be lined with bedding; the best type to buy is synthetic fleece. This is warm and cozy, and as moisture soaks through it, your puppy will not have a wet bed when he is tiny and still unable to go through the night without relieving himself. This type of bedding is machine washable and easy to dry. Buy two pieces, so you have one to use while the other piece is in the wash.

If you have a crate, you may not feel the need to buy a separate dog bed, although your Bulldog may like to have a bed in the family room so he feels part of household activities. There is an amazing array of dog-beds to chose from—beanbags, cushions, baskets, igloos, mini-four-posters—so you can take your pick! However, your Bulldog puppy may be destructive while he is teething, so hold off making a major investment until he has gone through the worst of the chewing phase.

Collar and leash

You may think that it is not worth buying a collar for the first few weeks, but the sooner your pup gets used to it, the better. A soft nylon collar is a good choice; it is lightweight and most puppies will accept it without making a fuss.

When your Bulldog matures, you will need a new collar. Now you might want to invest in a fancy leather one. Make sure the collar is comfortable around your Bulldog's neck, but not so loose that he can slip it off. Because sizing can be a problem, many owners opt for a harness, which works well with dogs who have a tendency to pull on the leash.

The leash can be leather or nylon, depending on personal preference. It should have a secure clip that is easy to take on and off.

Identification

Your Bulldog needs to wear some kind of ID when he is out and about. This can be in the form of a tag, engraved with your contact details, attached to the collar. When your Bulldog is full-grown, you can buy an embroidered collar with your contact details, which eliminates the danger of the disc becoming detached from the collar.

You may also wish to consider a permanent form of ID. Increasingly breeders are getting puppies microchipped before they go to their new homes. A microchip is the size of a grain of rice. It is injected under the skin, usually between the shoulder blades, with a special needle. It has some tiny barbs on it, which dig into the tissue around where it lies, so it does not migrate from that spot.

Each chip has its own unique identification number, which can only be read by a special scanner. That ID number is then registered with a national database, along with your name and contact details, so that if ever your dog is lost, he can be taken to any veterinarian or shelter, where he is scanned and then you are contacted. If your puppy has not been microchipped, you can ask your vet to do it, maybe when he goes for his vaccinations.

Bowls

Your Bulldog will need two bowls; one for food, and one for fresh drinking water, which should always be available.

A stainless steel bowl is a good choice, because it is tough and hygienic. Plastic bowls may be chewed, and there is a danger that bacteria can collect in the small cracks. Get a second stainless steel bowl for drinking water, or you may prefer a heavier ceramic bowl, which will not be knocked over so easily. Choose wide, shallow bowls that will accommodate your dog's broad muzzle.

Food

The breeder will let you know what your puppy is eating, and should provide a full diet sheet to guide you through the first six months—how many meals per day, how much he is eating per meal, when to increase the amounts given per meal, and when to reduce the meals per day.

The breeder may provide you with some food when you pick up your puppy, but it is worth asking in advance about the availability of the brand the breeder recommends.

Grooming gear

The Bulldog is a low-maintenance breed in terms of coat care, but there are a few essentials you will need to buy. These include:

- A soft nylon brush or a grooming mitt (a rubber glove with different size nodules on either side).
- Nail-clippers: guillotine-style clippers are easiest to use.
- Toothbrush and toothpaste made for dogs: a normal tooth-brush is adequate, and there are flavored canine toothpastes on the market that are great for dogs.
- Unscented alcohol-free wet wipes: use these to keep the face

folds clean, and also for cleaning under the tail. You can find these at most pet supply stores; these come in a resealable tub.

- Antiseptic powder and cream for the face folds. This may be specially manufactured for dogs, or you can use a diaper rash cream for infants.
- Medicated ear wipes: these will keep the ears fresh and clean.
- Petroleum jelly: to prevent the nose drying out.

Toys

There is a huge variety of toys to choose from, in a range of shapes, sizes, and materials. Your objective is not to buy the toy that looks the cutest, but to buy toys that are safe and that your dog will love. A Bulldog has powerful jaws, even when he is quite small, and he can be very destructive. Plastic toys can be shredded and soft toys can be chewed into little pieces.

If your dog swallows part of a toy, it could cause an obstruction, which could have lethal consequences. Avoid plastic toys and soft toys with squeakers; only offer soft toys if the eyes and nose have been removed.

The best toys for Bulldogs are hard rubber Kongs (which can be filled with food) and tough fabric tug toys. They may be more expensive, but safety comes first.

Finding a veterinarian

Pick out a local veterinarian before your puppy comes home. Visit some of the vets in your area, and speak to other pet owners to see who they recommend.

It is so important to find a good vet—as essential as finding a good doctor for yourself. You need to find someone you can build a good rapport with and have complete faith in. Word of mouth is really the best recommendation.

When you contact a veterinary practice, find out the following:

- Does the clinic have an appointment system? How far in advance can you make an appointment?
- What are the arrangements for emergency and after-hours coverage?
- Do any of the vets in the practice have experience treating Bulldogs?
- What facilities are available at the practice?

If you are satisfied with what you find, and the staff seem to be helpful and friendly, book an appointment for your puppy to have a health check a couple of days after you bring him home.

Settling in

When you first arrive home with your puppy, be careful not to overwhelm him. You and your family are hugely excited, but the puppy is in a completely strange environment with new sounds, smells, and sights, which is a daunting experience even for the boldest of pups.

Some puppies are very confident, wanting to play right away and quickly making friends; others need a little longer. Keep a close eye on your Bulldog's body language and reactions, so you can proceed at a pace he is comfortable with. Do not worry if he is a little unsure of himself at first, because this will not last long. In no time, he will be following you around, watching your every move.

First, let him explore the yard or the area just around your home. He will probably need to relieve himself after the journey home, so

take him to the designated toileting area, and when he performs give him plenty of praise. When you take your puppy indoors, let him investigate again.

Show him his crate, and encourage him to go in by throwing in a treat. Let him have a sniff, and allow him to go in and out as he wants to. Later on, when he is tired, you can put him in the crate while you stay in the room. In this way he will learn to settle down and will not think he is being abandoned.

It is a good idea to feed your puppy in his crate, at least to begin with, because this helps to build up a positive association. It will not be long before your Bulldog sees his crate as his own special den and will go there as a matter of choice. Some owners place a blanket over the crate, covering the back and sides, so it is even more cozy and den-like.

Meeting the family

Resist the temptation to invite friends and neighbors to come and meet the new arrival. For the first few days, your puppy needs to focus on getting to know his new family. Try not to swamp your Bulldog with too much attention; give him a chance to explore and find his feet. There will be plenty of time for cuddles later on!

If you have children in the family, you need to keep everything as calm as possible. Your puppy may not have met children before, and even if he has, he will still find them unpredictable. A puppy can become alarmed by too much noise, or go to the opposite extreme and become over-excited, which can lead to mouthing and nipping.

The best plan is to get the children to sit on the floor and give them each a dog treat. Each child can then call the puppy, pet him, and offer a treat. This way, the puppy is making the decisions rather than being forced into interactions he may find stressful.

Children should not regard the new puppy as a plaything, so do not leave them unattended with the pup until he has become less of a novelty. You need to supervise play so that neither the children nor the puppy become over-excited. Shouting, screaming, and running will be highly stimulating, and a puppy will react by chasing, jumping up, and maybe scratching by accident. You need to work at establishing calm interactions between your puppy and your children.

A puppy should not be tugged, pinched, or teased. If he is eating, he should not be disturbed. The same applies if he is resting in his bed or in his crate. Never allow a child to pick up a puppy, as it could result in serious injury or a broken limb if he is dropped.

The resident dog

If you already have an adult dog in the family, you will need to introduce your new puppy tactfully and supervise all their interactions to begin with. The yard or another neutral outdoor location is the best place for introducing the puppy, as there is more space and the adult will not feel as if his territory is being invaded.

He will probably take a great interest in the puppy and sniff him all over. Most puppies are naturally submissive in this situation;

your pup may lick the other dog's mouth or roll over on to his back. Try not to interfere, as this is the natural way dogs get to know each other.

As your Bulldog puppy settles into his new home, he will become increasingly confident so you will need to make sure that he does not take too many liberties with the older dog.

Feline friends

A Bulldog does not have a strong prey drive, but the curiosity of a puppy means a cat is a natural draw. However, harmonious relations can be established if you work at early interactions. You will need to progress step by step, making sure the pair are never left alone together until they have learned to ignore each other.

The real key to successful dog and cat introductions is to make sure the cat has plenty of high spaces to jump up out of reach of the dog. Feed kitty up high as well. And if it's a problem, put the litter box in a room blocked off from the puppy by a baby gate. The cat can easily jump over.

First meals

The breeder will typically provide enough food for the first few days, so the puppy does not have to cope with a change in diet—and possible digestive upset—along with all the stress of moving to a new home.

Some puppies polish off their food from the first meal onward; others are more concerned by their new surroundings and are too distracted to eat. Do not worry unduly if your puppy seems uninterested in his food for the first day or so. Give him 10 minutes to eat as much as he wants, and then remove the leftovers and start fresh at the next meal. (Obviously, if you have any concerns about your puppy in the first few days, seek advice from your veterinarian.)

The Bulldog is not the greediest eater, and you may find you have to tempt your pup a little when he first leaves the nest and does not have the competition of his siblings around him. A small amount of chicken or cheese sprinkled on his meal should be enough to tempt your puppy's appetite.

Bulldogs are not normally possessive about their food, but it is advisable to guard against this tendency from day one. If you have children, you need to establish a rule that no one is allowed to go near the dog when he is eating. This is plain common sense, and removes all risk of problems arising, no matter how unintentional.

At the same time, you can educate your Bulldog so he does not become stressed if people are around when he is eating. You can do this by giving him half his meal in his bowl, and then dropping some dry food around his bowl. This will stop him from guarding his bowl and, at the same time, he will see your presence in a positive way. You can also call him away from the bowl and reward him with some food that he can take from your hand. Start doing this as soon as your puppy arrives in his new home, and continue working on it throughout his life. Remember, food is a top priority for a dog; he will respect you as the provider, and if you interact with him as described, he will trust you and will not feel threatened.

The first night

Your puppy will have spent the first weeks of his life with either his mother or curled up with his siblings. He is then taken from everything he knows as familiar, lavished with attention by his new family—and then comes bed time when he is left all alone. It is little wonder he feels abandoned.

The best plan is to establish a routine right from the start, so your Bulldog becomes familiar with the ritual of going to his bed and settling until morning.

Take your puppy out to relieve himself, then encourage him to go into his crate. You can throw a couple of treats or biscuits in the crate, which will build up a good association with it, as well as diverting his attention while you close the door. Some people leave a night light on for the puppy for the first week, others have tried a radio as company or a ticking clock. A covered hot-water bottle filled with warm water can also be a comfort. Like people, puppies are all individuals, and what works for one does not necessarily work for another, so it is a matter of trial and error.

Be very positive when you leave your puppy on his own. Do not linger or keep returning; this will make the situation more difficult. It is inevitable that he will protest to begin with, but if you stick to your routine, he will accept that he gets left at night—but you always return in the morning.

Rescued dogs

Settling an older, rescued dog in the home is very similar to what you'd do with a puppy. You will need to buy the same items and make the same preparations for his homecoming. As with a puppy, with an adult dog will appreciate consistency, so start as you mean to go on. There is often an initial honeymoon period when you bring home a rescued dog, and he may be on his best behavior for the first few weeks. It is after these first couple of weeks that the true nature of the dog will show, so be prepared for subtle changes. It may be advisable to sign up for training classes, so you can seek advice on any training or behavioral issues at an early stage.

Above all, remember that a rescued dog ceases to be a rescued

dog the moment he enters his forever home, and should be treated like any other family dog.

Housetraining

This is the aspect of training that puppy owners dread. But it doesn't have to be an ordeal if you put in the time and effort in the first few weeks. The key to successful housetraining is vigilance and consistency. If you establish a routine and stick to it, your puppy will understand what is required.

Equally, you must be there to supervise him at all times—except when he is safely tucked in his crate. It is when a puppy is left to wander from room to room that accidents are most likely to happen.

As discussed earlier, you will have allocated a toileting area outside when preparing for your puppy's homecoming. You must take your puppy to this area every time he needs to relieve himself, so he builds up an association and knows why you have brought him out.

Establish a routine and make sure you take your puppy out at the following times:

- First thing in the morning
- After mealtimes
- Whenever he wakes from a nap
- After a play session
- Last thing at night

A puppy should be taken out to relieve himself every two hours as an absolute minimum. If you can manage an hourly trip, so much the better. The more often your puppy gets it right, the quicker he will learn to be clean in the house. It helps if you use a verbal cue, such as "Busy," when your pup is performing, and in time, this will trigger the desired response.

Do not be tempted to put your puppy out on the doorstep in the hope that he will toilet on his own. Most pups simply sit there, waiting to get back inside the house! No matter how bad the weather is, accompany your puppy and give him lots of praise when he performs correctly.

Do not rush back inside as soon as he has finished. Your puppy might start to delay in the hope of prolonging his time outside with you. Praise him, have a quick game—and then you can both return indoors.

When accidents happen

No matter how vigilant you are, there are bound to be accidents. If you witness the accident, just interrupt him by calling his name, then take your puppy outside immediately. Give him lots of praise if he finishes his business out there.

If you are not there when he has an accident, do not scold him when you discover what has happened. He will not remember what he has done and will not understand why you are angry with him. Simply clean it up and resolve to be more vigilant next time.

Make sure you use an enzymatic cleaner made specifically for pet messes when you clean up. Otherwise, your pup will be drawn to the smell and may be tempted to use the same spot again.

Choosing a diet

Providing a well-balanced, good-quality diet is of paramount importance, as this is the key to owning a healthy dog. There are lots of different diets to choose from, and you will need to think about convenience, availability and, most importantly, what is best for your dog.

Many people feed puppy foods, which are formulated to support growth, for the first year of a puppy's life, and then switch to adult foods.

No matter what diet you ultimately choose, start off with the same food the breeder fed your pup. He's experiencing a lot of changes all at once—food doesn't have to be one of them. After a few weeks, you can start gradually transitioning him to the food you've chosen.

Dry food

Most dry foods, or kibble, are scientifically formulated to meet all your dog's nutritional needs. Kibble is certainly convenient, and if often less expensive than other diets.

There are many brands of kibble available, and most offer life-stage foods, such as puppy, adult, and senior. There are also special diets for pregnant bitches, working dogs, and prescription diets for weight control, and other health-related conditions.

Which kibble is best? This is a difficult question, but the best plan is to seek advice from your puppy's breeder or your veterinarian. When choosing a complete diet, opt for larger size kibble as a Bulldog can drop small pieces from the side of his mouth as he eats.

Kibble can be fed on its own, or along with other types of food. It is best fed in a puzzle toy—a toy dogs must manipulate in some way to get the food out. No dog is too young—or too old!—to start eating kibble from a puzzle toy.

Canned food

Canned food contains a lot more water than kibble. Some canned foods—although certainly not all—will have fewer carbohydrates than kibble. Read the label carefully so you are aware of the ingredients and, remember, what you put in will affect what comes out.

Canned food can be all or part of your dog's diet. Even if it is only a part, the label should say the diet is complete and balanced for your dog.

Raw diets

Raw diets may come fresh or frozen or freeze-dried, or you might choose to prepare your dog's diet yourself. They typically contain raw meat, bones, organ meats, fat, vegetables, and sometimes, some cooked grains. Proponents of raw diets believe they are providing

the dog with a food that is very close to the natural diet if she would eat in the wild.

If you're buying a raw diet, look for a statement on the label that says it's complete and balanced. If you want to prepare the diet yourself, work with a veterinary nutritionist to formulate a healthy diet for your dog. There are a lot of raw diet recipes on the Internet, but recent research has found that the majority of them do not offer complete and balanced nutrition.

A feeding schedule

Most pups at eat four meals a day, depending on the appetite of the individual. It is sensible to stick to the schedule recommended by the breeder for the first few weeks.

When he is around 15 weeks, you can cut out one of his meals; he may well have started to leave some of his food, indicating he is ready to do this. By six months, he can move on to two meals a day—a regime that will likely suit him for the rest of his life.

Do not feed your dog before exercise or immediately afterward as this can result in a potentially lethal condition called bloat (more about that in chapter 9). Make sure you leave an hour, at minimum, before and after meals.

Picky eaters

Bulldogs are not always the most enthusiastic eaters, and it is tempting to try to entice your dog to eat. One look from those dark eyes is enough to melt your heart, stirring you to greater efforts to find a food that he will really like.

At first you may add some gravy, then you may try some chicken. The clever Bulldog will quickly realize that if he holds out, tastier treats will follow. If your dog is turning up his nose at mealtimes, give him 10 minutes to eat what he wants, then pick up his bowl and give him fresh food at his next meal.

Do not feed him treats in between meals. If you continue this for a couple of days, your Bulldog will realize that there is nothing to gain in holding out for better food, because nothing else will be coming. In most cases, if you approach his pickiness with common sense, your Bulldog will be content with the food you have chosen for him.

If, however, your dog refuses all food for more than 24 hours, you need to observe his behavior to see if there are any signs of ill health, including dental problems, which may indicate a need for a veterinary check-up.

Bones and chews

Puppies love to chew, and many adult dogs also enjoy gnawing on a bone. Bones should always be hard and uncooked; rib bones and poultry bones must be avoided, because they can splinter and cause major problems.

Dental chews and some of the manufactured rawhide chews are safe, but they should be given only under supervision.

Ideal weight

With his relatively short legs and powerfully built body, it is not always easy to detect when your Bulldog is putting on weight. And with a breed that does not believe in strenuous exercise, it is all too easy to give your dog more food than he needs.

Obesity is a major problem in Bulldogs, and this can have devastating effects not only on your dog's quality of life but also on his longevity. An overweight dog will become lethargic and will cease to engage in family activities because it is all too much effort.

His health will also be affected; overweight dogs are prone to heart conditions, diabetes, joint problems, and digestive disorders. Your dog's life expectancy will be seriously shortened if he is even moderately obese.

When judging your Bulldog's condition, look at him from above, and make sure you can see a definite waist. You should be able to feel his ribs but not see them.

If you are concerned about your Bulldog's weight, get into the habit of visiting the veterinary clinic monthly so that you can weigh him. They should allow you to stop by for this at no charge. You can keep a record of his weight, and adjust his meals if necessary.

Chapter 6

Caring for Your Bulldog

The short-haired Bulldog is low-maintenance in terms of coat care, but like all breeds she has her own special needs. These are now your responsibility as a Bulldog owner.

Puppy care

When your Bulldog puppy first arrives in her new home at around 10 to 12 weeks of age, she will need little in the way of coat care. But it's really important that she gets used to being handled. Throughout her life she will need to be groomed, have routine preventive health care, and, on occasion, she will need to be examined by a veterinarian. If she is accustomed to handling from an early age, there will be no need for stress and fuss over routine care.

Start by handling your puppy all over, stroking her from her head to her tail. Lift up each paw in turn, and reward her with a treat when she cooperates. Then roll her over on her back and tickle

her tummy; this is a very vulnerable position for a dog, so do not force the issue. Be firm but gentle, and give your puppy lots of praise when she does as you ask.

Adult grooming

The Bulldog's short, smooth coat requires minimal of grooming, but that doesn't mean you can just neglect it. Remember that as well as keeping the coat in good condition, grooming is a kind of massage and aids circulation. It also gives you the opportunity to check your Bulldog for any sore places or unusual lumps or bumps. Problems spotted at an early stage are always easier to treat.

Spend a few minutes brushing the coat every day, using a soft body brush. If you want your dog's coat to shine, you can give her a wipe over with a piece of chamois or silk.

Some Bulldog owners also use a spray-on conditioner to keep the coat at its best. Bulldogs do shed their coats; in centrally heated houses this tends to be an ongoing process rather than a seasonal shed. If you feel your Bulldog is shedding more than normal, you can use a shedding blade to help get rid of the dead hair.

Routine care

As well as looking after her coat, your Bulldog will need regular care to keep her healthy and prevent problems. Make her care part of your daily and weekly routine.

Grooming provides an opportunity to give your Bulldog a thorough check-up.

Nail trimming does not need to be a battle! Start young, and offer plenty of encouragement and rewards.

The folds on your dog's face must be kept clean and dry. Make this a daily habit and you will avoid a lot of problems.

Facial care

The Bulldog's wrinkles are a characteristic of the breed; they make a Bulldog look like a Bulldog. Modern breeders should steer clear of exaggeration, and so this feature should not be overdone. But even modest wrinkling needs daily attention. If the skin between the wrinkles becomes moist, soreness and infection can easily develop.

You need to use unscented wipes (with no alcohol!) to clean the skin. Then dry it with cotton balls, and apply a medicated skin powder or cornstarch-based powder. If the skin looks red or inflamed, apply a diaper rash cream or an over-the-counter antibiotic cream.

Remember, you must clean your Bulldog's face every day. You will be shocked at how quickly sore spots develop if you don't.

Eyes

Your Bulldog's eyes should appear bright, clear, and clean. You can buy special eye wipes that can be used to clean "sleep" discharge that can be present in the morning.

Some Bulldogs are prone to tear-staining; if this is the case with your Bulldog, use unscented wipes to clean the face. Staining can be kept to a minimum if you apply a small pinch of boric powder, which you can buy at a drugstore. If your Bulldog's eyes look red or inflamed, or if there is evidence of discharge, you should make an appointment with the veterinarian right away.

Ears

During your regular grooming session, inspect your Bulldog's ears to make sure they are clean and don't have an odor. There are several brands of ear cleaner you can find at your pet supply store. Follow the directions on the bottle. If you notice your Bulldog scratching her ears, shaking her head, or holding her head to one side, make an appointment to see the veterinarian.

Tail

The Bulldog's tail naturally varies in size and length, and may be straight or screwed.

Keep a close check on the tail area to ensure it is clean and free from hair, which could be an irritation. If the tail is clamped tight to the anus—now considered a fault in the breed—use diaper rash cream to prevent problems.

Teeth

Dental disease is increasing among dogs, so teeth cleaning should be part of your care regime. A buildup of tartar on the teeth can result in tooth decay, gum infection, and bad breath. If it is allowed to accumulate, you may have no option but to get the teeth cleaned under anesthesia.

When your Bulldog is still a puppy, get him used to having his teeth brushed. It becomes just another routine. Dog toothpaste comes in a variety of meaty flavors that your Bulldog will like. (Never use toothpaste for humans on your dog!) You can start by putting toothpaste on your finger and gently rubbing his teeth. You can then progress to using a finger brush or a toothbrush—whichever you find most convenient. Remember to reward your Bulldog when she cooperates, and she will positively look forward to her teeth-brushing sessions.

Nails

Nail trimming is a task dreaded by many owners—and many dogs—but, again, if you start early, your Bulldog will get used to it and will not fuss. Clip just one or two nails at first, and be sure to offer plenty of praise and treats.

Depending on her color, your Bulldog may have white or black nails. In a white nail you can see the quick—the vein that runs through the nail—but this is obscured in black nails. For this reason, only trim the tips of the nails so you don't cut into the quick. If you do this inadvertently, it is not disastrous, but it will cause the nail to bleed profusely. This will be uncomfortable for your Bulldog and she will remember it next time you attempt to trim her nails.

If you are worried about trimming your Bulldog's nails, ask your dog's breeder or veterinarian to show you how to do it properly. If you are still concerned, you can always use the services of a professional groomer.

Exercise

The Bulldog enjoys going out and about. She loves the opportunity to use her nose and to discover new places. She does not need as much exercise as the working and sporting breeds, but do not neglect this aspect of her care. A fit Bulldog will enjoy a longer, healthier life.

The Bulldog is heavy for her size, so you need to limit exercise during the vulnerable growing period. Time in the yard, short leash-walking expeditions for socialization, and 10-minute off-leash sessions are plenty for the first 12 months. Bulldogs who are over-exercised while they are growing can damage their joints and they also risk bone distortion.

The adult Bulldog will appreciate daily outings, and the more variety you can provide, the better. Most Bulldogs have a burst of activity—particularly young, adolescent dogs—and then take things at their own pace. Some enjoy retrieving games or playing hide-and-seek, which provides mental stimulation as well as physical exercise.

The older Bulldog

The Bulldog is not the most long-lived of breeds—the average life expectancy is 8 to 10 years—so you need to take the greatest care of your dog when she starts to age. The timing of this will vary, but there is no doubt that a fit dog, kept at the correct weight, will live longer and better. The older Bulldog may sleep more and may be reluctant to go for longer walks. She may show signs of stiffness when she gets up, but these generally ease when she starts moving. Some older Bulldogs may have impaired vision, and some become a little deaf, but as long as their senses do not deteriorate dramatically, this is something they learn to live with.

It is advisable to switch her over to a senior diet, which is more

suited to her needs. You may need to feed a bit less, because she will not be burning up the calories she did when she was younger.

Make sure her sleeping quarters are warm and draft-free, and if she gets wet, make sure you dry her thoroughly. Most important of all, be guided by your Bulldog. She will have good days when she feels up to going for a walk, and other days when she would prefer to amble around in the yard or close to home.

If you have a younger dog at home, this may stimulate your Bulldog to take more of an interest in what is going on. But make sure she is not pestered, as she needs to rest undisturbed when she is tired.

Letting go

Inevitably there comes a time when your Bulldog is not enjoying a good quality of life, and you need to make the painful decision to let her go. We all wish that our dogs died painlessly in their sleep, but unfortunately, this is rarely the case. However, we can allow our dogs to die with dignity, and to suffer as a little as possible. This should be our way of saying thank you for the wonderful companionship they have given us.

When you feel the time is near, talk to your vet, who will be able to make an objective assessment of your Bulldog's condition and will help you to make the right decision.

This is the hardest thing you will ever have to do as a dog owner, and it is only natural to grieve for your beloved Bulldog. But eventually, you will be able to look back with sweetness on the happy memories of times spent together. And you may, in time, realize that your life is not complete without another Bulldog.

Chapter 7

Understanding and Training Your Bulldog

T
o live in the modern world without fears and anxieties, your Bulldog needs to receive an education in social skills, so he learns to cope calmly and confidently in a wide variety of situations. The Bulldog is a naturally sociable and outgoing dog, but you need to maximize his learning opportunities, particularly in the first 12 months of his life.

Early learning

Your puppy's breeder will have begun a program of socialization by getting their puppies used to all the sights and sounds of a busy household. You need to continue this when your pup arrives in his

new home. To begin with, your puppy needs to get used to all the members of his new family; then you should give him the opportunity to meet other people who come to the house. If you do not have children of your own, make sure your puppy has the chance to meet and play with other people's children—making sure interactions are always supervised—so he learns that humans come in small sizes, too.

You also need to make sure he is not bothered by household appliances, such as the vacuum cleaner or the washing machine, and that he gets used to unexpected noises from the television and computers.

The outside world

When your puppy has completed his vaccinations, he is ready to venture into the outside world. As a breed, the Bulldog is pretty laid back, but there is a lot for a youngster to take on board, so do not swamp him with too many new experiences when you first set out.

Obviously, you need to work at leash training before your first expedition. There will be plenty of distractions, so you do not want additional problems of coping with a dog who is pulling or lagging on the leash. Start in your backyard or close to home, with your Bulldog walking by your side on a loose leash. He may need additional encouragement when you venture farther afield, so arm yourself with some extra special treats, which will give him a good reason to focus on you when required! (You'll find more about leash training later in this chapter.)

Start socializing your puppy in a quiet area with light traffic, and only progress to a busier place when he is ready. There is so much to see and hear—people (maybe carrying bags or umbrellas), wheelchairs, strollers, bicycles, cars, trucks—so give your puppy a chance to take it all in.

If he does seem worried, do not fall into the trap of sympathizing with or reassuring him, or worse still, picking him up. This will only teach your pup that he had a good reason to be worried and, with luck, you will "rescue" him whenever he feels scared.

Instead, give him a little space so he does not have to confront whatever he is frightened of, and distract him with a few treats. Then encourage him to walk past, using an upbeat tone of voice. Never force him by yanking on the leash. Reward him for any forward movement, and your puppy will soon learn that he can trust you and there is nothing to fear.

Dog meets dog

Your pup also needs to continue his education, started by his mother and by his litter mates, in canine manners. He needs to be able to greet all dogs calmly, giving the signals that say he is friendly and offers no threat.

This is especially important with a Bulldog as his unique appearance can be his downfall. Dogs use body language and facial expressions to communicate with one another, but most breeds struggle to read what is going on with the Bulldog. His large head, massive undershot jaw, and wrinkles give him a particular look that we humans love, but that can be baffling to other dogs. Added to this, the Bulldog's barrel shape and lack of tail means signaling through body language is limited.

If a dog is unsure or even fearful when meeting a Bulldog, he may become assertive simply because he doesn't know what else to do. A Bulldog may well start off with good intentions, but if he senses the other's dog's uncertainty and suspicion, he may become reactive. The Bulldog's fighting instincts, born from his ancestry as a bull-baiting dog, are hugely diluted, but if he feels threatened, he will look after himself—and this could be a problem.

Therefore, it is important that your Bulldog learns to give off good vibes, greeting dogs calmly and quietly so they have nothing to worry about. Here's a way to do it.

Find a friend who has a dog with a bulletproof temperament and visit their house. Allow the two dogs to play in the yard for 10 minutes or so. Do not prolong the game, as you do not want your youngster to become over-excited or overwhelmed.

After the two dogs have had a few play-dates at home, go for a walk and allow them to exercise together in a safe place off leash. They will interact with each other, but their focus will shift periodically as they become distracted by other sights and smells.

Now extend your Bulldog's social circle by finding other friends who have dogs of sound temperament. The more your Bulldog practices meeting and greeting, the better he will become at reading body language and assessing other dogs' intentions.

Training classes

A training class will give your Bulldog the opportunity to work alongside other dogs in a controlled situation, and he will also learn to focus on you in a different, distracting environment. Both these lessons will be vital as your dog matures.

However, the training class needs to be really well run or you risk doing more harm than good. Before you go along with your puppy, attend a class as an observer to make sure you are happy with what goes on. Find out the following:

- How much training experience do the instructors have?
- Are the classes divided into appropriate age categories?
- Do they use only positive, reward-based training methods?
- Do any of the instructors have experience with Bulldogs?

If the training class is well run, it is certainly worth attending. Both you and your Bulldog will learn useful training exercises. It

will increase his social skills, and you will have the chance to talk to lots of like-minded dog enthusiasts.

Training guidelines

Dog training advice

The Bulldog is a thinking dog and, while there is no doubting his intelligence, he may be reluctant to cooperate if he doesn't see the point of what you are asking him to do. It is therefore important to keep training sessions both short and positive, with lots of rewards to keep him fully motivated.

You will be eager to get started (and in fact, dogs are learning every moment they are with you), but in your rush to start on a training program, don't forget the fundamentals that could make the difference between success and failure.

You need to get into the mindset of a Bulldog, working out what makes him tick and, equally, what makes him switch off. Decide on your priorities for training, set realistic goals, and then think of ways to make your training as effective and as fun as possible.

Providing a worthwhile reward is an essential tool in training. You will probably get the best results if you use some extra special food treats, such as cheese or cooked meat. Some Bulldogs will work for a toy, but they are the exception rather than the rule. If you decide to use a toy, make sure you bring it out only for training sessions, so it gains extra value.

Keep your verbal cues simple, and always use the same one for each exercise. For example, when you ask your puppy to go into the Down position, the cue is "Down," not "Lie Down," Get Down," or anything else. Remember, your Bulldog does not speak English; he associates the sound of the word with the action.

Here are some other guidelines to keep in mind when you start training.

- Choose an area that is free from distractions, so your puppy will focus on you. You can progress to a more challenging environment as your pup progresses.
- Do not train your puppy just after he has eaten or exercised. He will either be too full or too tired to concentrate.
- Do not train if you are in a bad mood, or if you are short of time; those sessions always end in disaster!
- Never introduce a verbal cue until your dog clearly understands the exercise.
- If your dog is finding an exercise difficult, break it down into small steps so it is easier to understand. The Bulldog can be stubborn, and if he becomes frustrated he may decide to just stop working.
- Do not make your training sessions boring and repetitious. Your Bulldog will be quick to lose interest if there are no tangible rewards.
- Do not train for too long, particularly with a young puppy who has a very short attention span.

- Always end training sessions on a positive note. This does not necessarily mean getting an exercise right. If your pup is making mistakes, ask him to do a simple exercise so you have the opportunity to praise and reward him.
- Remember that if your Bulldog is rewarded for a behavior, he is likely to repeat it—so make sure you are 100 percent consistent and always reward the behavior you want to see.

First lessons

Like all puppies, a young Bulldog will soak up new experiences like a sponge, so training should start from the time your pup arrives in his new home.

Wearing a collar

You may or may not want your Bulldog to wear a collar all the time. But when he goes out in public he will need to be on a leash, and so he should get used to the feel of a collar around his neck. The best plan is to accustom your pup to wearing a soft collar for a few minutes at a time, until he forgets about it.

Fit the collar so that you can get at least two fingers between the collar and his neck. Then have a game to distract his attention. This will work for a few moments; then he will stop, put his back leg up behind his neck, and scratch away at the peculiar thing around his neck.

Bend down, rotate the collar, pat him on the head, and distract him by playing with a toy or giving him a treat. When he has worn the collar for a few minutes each day, he will soon ignore it.

Remember, never leave the collar on an unsupervised puppy, especially when he is out in the yard or when he is in his crate, as it is could get snagged, causing serious injury.

Walking on the leash

This is a simple exercise, but the Bulldog can be a little stubborn. It's a good idea to master the basics at home before venturing into the outside world where there is so much to distract him.

When your puppy is used to the collar, take him outside into your secure yard or to a quiet spot outside where there are no distractions. Attach the leash and, to begin with, allow him to wander with the leash trailing, making sure it does not become snagged.

Then pick up the leash and follow the pup where he wants to go;

he needs to get used to the sensation of being attached to you.

The next step is to get your Bulldog to follow you, and for this you will need some treats. To give yourself the best chance of success, make sure the treats are high value—cheese, sausage, or whatever he really adores—so your Bulldog is motivated to work with you.

Show him you have a treat in your hand, then encourage him to follow you. Walk a few paces, and if he is walking with you, stop and reward him. If he puts on the brakes, simply change direction and lure him with the treat.

Next, introduce some changes of direction so your puppy is walking confidently alongside you. At this stage, introduce a verbal cue "Heel" when your puppy is in the correct position.

You can then graduate to walking your puppy away from home, starting in quiet areas and building up to busier environments.

Leash training strategies

The Bulldog is a strong, muscular dog, and any tendency to pull on the leash should be discouraged. It is unpleasant for you, and puts pressure on your dog's respiratory system as he strains against you. Your dog needs to learn, right from the start, that there is absolutely no advantage to pulling.

Restrict leash training to the yard or a safe fenced area in the initial stages so you are working in an environment that is free from distractions. Walk a few paces, being very aware of any tension on the leash. If you feel the leash tighten and your Bulldog is attempting to get ahead of you, stop, change direction, and set off again.

Your Bulldog needs to understand that pulling ahead has exactly the opposite effect from he wants. Rather than calling the shots, he has to cooperate with you.

Keep a good supply of tasty treats and remember, only reward—with food and with verbal praise—when he is walking on a loose leash by your side. The mistake many owners make at this stage is to use the treats to lure the dog into position, rather than rewarding him for the correct behavior. Have the patience to wait until he gets it right on his own (and with some verbal encouragement from you), and then offer him the reward.

Keep training sessions short, and when you are ready to venture into the outside world, do not be too ambitious to begin with. Build up the level of distractions and the duration of leash walking only when your Bulldog is consistently showing the behavior you want.

Come when called

The key to successful recall training is to start early, and to teach your Bulldog to focus on you, regardless of temptations.

Hopefully, the breeder will have laid the foundations simply by calling the puppies to "Come" when it is time to eat, and when they are moving from one place to another. You can build on this when your puppy arrives in his new home, calling him to "Come" when he is in a confined space, such as the kitchen. This is a good place to build up a positive association with the verbal cue—particularly if you ask your puppy to "Come" to get his meals!

The next stage is to transfer the lesson outside. Arm yourself with some treats, and wait until your puppy is distracted. Then call him, using a higher-pitched, excited tone of voice. At this stage, a puppy wants to be with you, so capitalize on this and keep practicing the verbal cue and rewarding your puppy with a treat and lots of praise when he comes to you.

Now you are ready to introduce some distractions. Try calling him when someone else is nearby, or wait a few minutes until he is investigating a really interesting scent. When he responds, make a big fuss over him and give him some extra treats so he knows it is worth his while to come to you.

If he is slow to come, run away a few steps and then call again, making yourself sound really exciting. Jump up and down, open your arms wide to welcome him. It doesn't matter how silly you look; he needs to see you as the most fun person in the world.

When you have a reliable recall in the yard, you can venture into the outside world. Do not be too ambitious to begin with; try a recall in a quiet place with minimal distractions, so you can be assured of success.

Do not make the mistake of asking your dog to come only when it's time to end a walk or play time or something else he enjoys. What is the incentive in coming back to you if all you do is clip on his leash and end his free time? Instead, call your dog at random times, giving him a treat and a pat, and then letting him go free again. In this way, coming to you—and focusing on you—is always rewarding.

Stationary exercises

The Sit and Down are easy to teach, and mastering these exercises will be rewarding for both you and your Bulldog. They are useful in a wide variety of situations and ensure you always have a way to control your dog.

Sit

The best way to teach this cue is to lure your Bulldog into position, and for this you can use a treat or his food bowl. Hold the reward (a treat or food bowl) above his head. As he looks up, he will lower his hindquarters and automatically sit. Give him his treat.

Practice this a few times and when your puppy understands what you are asking, introduce the verbal cue, "Sit."

When your Bulldog understands the exercise, he will respond to the verbal cue alone, and you will not need to reward him every time he sits. However, it is a good idea to give him a treat on a random basis when he cooperates to keep him guessing!

Down

This is an important lesson, and can be a lifesaver if there's an emergency and you need your Bulldog to stop instantly.

You can start with

your dog sitting or standing for this exercise. Stand or kneel in front of him and show him you have a treat in your hand. Hold the treat just in front of his nose and slowly lower it to the ground between his front legs.

As your Bulldog follows the treat, he will go down on his front legs and, in a few moments, his hindquarters will follow. Close your hand over the treat so he doesn't cheat and get the treat before he is in the correct position. As soon as he is in the Down position, give him the treat and lots of praise.

Keep practicing, and when your Bulldog understands what you want, introduce the verbal cue "Down."

Control exercises

These exercises may not be the most exciting, but they are important in establishing a relationship of mutual respect with your Bulldog.

Wait

This exercise teaches your Bulldog to wait in position until you give the next cue. It's different from the Stay exercise, where he must stay where you have left him for a longer time. The most useful application of Wait is when you are getting your dog out of the car and you need him to stay in position until you clip on his leash.

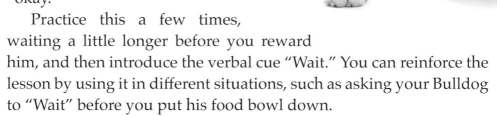

Start with your puppy on the leash to give you a greater chance of success. Ask him to "Sit," and stand in front him. Step back one pace, holding your hand, palm flat, facing him. Wait a second, and then come back to stand in front of him. You can then reward him and release him with a word, such as "okay."

Practice this a few times, waiting a little longer before you reward him, and then introduce the verbal cue "Wait." You can reinforce the lesson by using it in different situations, such as asking your Bulldog to "Wait" before you put his food bowl down.

Stay

You need to differentiate this exercise from the Wait by using a different hand signal and a different verbal cue.

Start with your Bulldog in the Down, as he is most likely to be secure in this position. Stand by his side and then step forward with your hand held back, palm facing the dog. Step back, release him, and then reward him. Practice until your Bulldog understands the exercise. Then introduce the verbal cue "Stay."

Gradually increase the distance you can leave your puppy, and increase the challenge by walking around him—and even stepping over him—so that he learns he must "Stay" until you release him.

Leave it

This is a useful cue for teaching your Bulldog to give up a toy on request, and it follows that he will give up anything when he is asked—which is very useful if he has got hold of a forbidden object or a piece of rotten garbage in the street.

This is an important cue to help your Bulldog learn to cooperate with you. Bulldogs have a tendency to guard resources they see as being valuable; this can be food, toys, or a comfortable sofa or bed. You therefore need to teach your Bulldog to give up things he values without forcing the issue and provoking conflict.

The "Leave it" cue can be taught quite easily when you are first playing with your puppy. As you gently take a toy from his mouth, introduce the verbal cue, "Leave it," and then praise him.

If he is reluctant, swap the toy for another toy or a treat. This will usually do the trick.

Do not try to pull the toy from his mouth if he refuses to give it up, as you will make the situation confrontational. Let the toy go "dead" in your hand, and then, when he drops it, swap it for a new toy or a really high-value treat, so this becomes the better option.

Remember to make a big fuss over your Bulldog when he does as you ask, so he learns that cooperation is always the best—and most rewarding—option.

Chapter 8

Keeping Your Bulldog Busy

The Bulldog is an outstanding companion—and she sees this as her main career. She is not ambitious in terms of competing in sporting activities, but if you are prepared to take it slow and steady and have reasonable expectations, she may surprise you!

Agility

Agility (shown in the photo opposite) is basically a canine obstacle course. It is fast and furious and is great for the fitness of both handler and dog. And it can be quite addictive! The obstacles include hurdles, long jump, tire jump, tunnels (rigid and collapsible), weaving poles, an A-frame, a dog-walk, and a seesaw.

This is not a natural sport for a Bulldog as she does not have the conformation to run quickly around an agility course. However, she can have a go at fun agility, jumping at a low height, and going through tunnels. Training clubs often run fun agility classes. Puppies

should not be allowed to do any agility exercises that involve jumping or contact equipment until they are at least 12 months old.

Canine Good Citizen

The American Kennel Club runs the Canine Good Citizen program. It promotes responsible ownership and helps you to train a well-behaved dog who will fit in with the community.

The program tests your dog on basic good manners, alone and with other people and dogs around. It's excellent for all pet owners and is also an ideal starting point if you plan to compete with your Bulldog in any sport when she is older.

Obedience

If your Bulldog masters the basic obedience of the Canine Good Citizen, you may want to get involved in competitive obedience. The

exercises include heelwork at varying paces with dog and handler following a pattern decided by the judge, stays, recalls, retrieves, sendaways, scent discrimination, and distance control. The exercises get progressively harder as you move through the classes.

With patience and lots of rewards, a Bulldog will learn the exercises that are in obedience competitions. However, this is a discipline that calls for a very high degree of precision and accuracy, which does not suit all dogs—or all handlers.

Rally O

This sport is loosely based on obedience, and also has a few exercises borrowed from agility when you get to the highest levels. Handler and dog must complete a course, in the designated order, that has a variety of different exercises. The course is timed and the team must complete within the time limit that is set, but there are no bonus marks for speed.

The great advantage of Rally O is that it is very relaxed, and anyone can compete. In fact, it has proved very popular for handlers with disabilities, as they are able to work their dogs to a high standard and compete on equal terms with other competitors.

Showing

Exhibiting at a dog show may seem easy, but it requires a lot of training and preparation, particularly when you are showing a strong-minded, heavyweight breed. Still, showing is a great way to meet other Bulldog lovers, even if you never take home the a ribbon.

Your Bulldog will have to be calm and confident in the busy show atmosphere, so you need to work on her socialization, and also take her to ringcraft classes so you both learn what is required at a show. She will be subjected to a detailed hands-on examination by the judge; she must learn to stand still in a show pose and to move on a loose leash so the judge can assess her gait.

Chapter 9

Health Care
for Bulldogs

Your Bulldog depends on you for all his needs—food, shelter, and health care. Keeping your dog healthy is not just about taking him to the vet when he is unwell, it is about putting a program of preventive health care in place. This should start from the moment your dog arrives in his new home.

Parasites

No matter how well you look after your Bulldog, you will have to accept that parasites—internal and external—are ever present, and you need to take preventive action.

Internal parasites live inside your dog. These are the various worms. Most will find a home in the digestive tract, but there is also a parasite that lives in the heart. If infestation is unchecked, a dog's health will be severely jeopardized, but routine preventive treatment is simple and effective.

External parasites live on your dog's body—in his skin and fur, and sometimes in his ears.

Roundworm

This is found in the small intestine. Signs of infestation will be a poor coat, a potbelly, diarrhea, and lethargy. Prospective mothers should be treated before mating, but it is almost inevitable that parasites she may have will be passed on to the puppies. For this rea-

Vaccinating Your Dog

The American Animal Hospital Association and the American Veterinary Medical Association have issued vaccination guidelines that apply to all breeds of dogs. They divide the available vaccines into two groups: core vaccines, which every dog should get, and non-core vaccines, which are optional.

Core vaccines are canine parvovirus-2, distemper, and adenovirus-2. Puppies should get vaccinated every three to four weeks between the ages of 6 and 16 weeks, with the final dose at 14 to 16 weeks of age. If a dog older than 16 weeks is getting their first vaccine, one dose is enough. Dogs who received an initial dose at less than 16 weeks should be given a booster after one year, and then every three years or more thereafter.

Rabies is also a core vaccine. For puppies less than 16 weeks old, a single dose should be given no earlier than 12 weeks of age. Revaccination is recommended annually or every three years, depending on the vaccine used and state and local laws.

Non-core vaccines are canine parainfluenza virus, Bordetella bronchiseptica, canine influenza virus, canine measles, leptospirosis, and Lyme disease. The dog's exposure risk, lifestyle, and geographic location all come into play when deciding which non-core vaccines may be appropriate for your dog. Have a conversation with your veterinarian about the right vaccine protocol for your dog.

son, a breeder will start a worming program, which you will need to continue. Ask your vet for advice on treatment, which will need to continue throughout your dog's life.

Tapeworm

Infection occurs when the dog ingests fleas or lice. The adult worm takes up residence in the small intestine, releasing mobile segments (which contain eggs), which can be seen in a dog's feces as small rice-like grains. The only other obvious sign of infestation is irritation of the anus. Again, routine preventive treatment is required throughout your dog's life.

Heartworm

This parasite is transmitted by mosquitoes, and is found in all parts of the USA, although its prevalence does vary. Heartworms live in the right side of the heart and larvae can grow up to 14 inches (35 cm) long. A dog with heartworm is at severe risk from heart failure, so preventive treatment, as advised by your vet, is essential. Dogs should also have regular tests to check for the presence of infection.

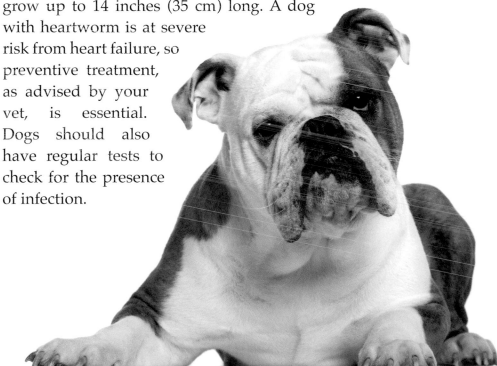

Lungworm

Lungworm is a parasite that lives in the heart and major blood vessels supplying the lungs. It can cause many problems, such as breathing difficulties, excessive bleeding, sickness, diarrhea, seizures, and even death. The dog becomes infected when ingesting slugs and snails, often accidentally when rummaging through undergrowth. Lungworm is not common, but it is on the increase and a responsible owner should be aware of it. Fortunately, it is easily preventable, and even affected dogs usually make a full recovery if treated early enough. Your vet will be able to advise you on the risks in your area and what form of treatment may be required.

How to Detect Fleas

You may suspect your dog has fleas, but how can you be sure? There are two methods to try. Run a fine comb through your dog's coat, and see if you can detect the presence of fleas on the skin or clinging to the comb. Alternatively, sit your dog on some white paper and rub his back. This will dislodge feces from the fleas, which will be visible as small brown specks. To double check, shake the specks on to some damp cotton. Flea feces consists of the dried blood taken from the host, so if the specks turn a lighter shade of red, you know your dog has fleas.

Fleas

A dog may carry many types of fleas. The flea stays on the dog only long enough to feed and breed, but its presence will result in itching. If your dog has an allergy to fleas—usually a reaction to the flea's saliva—she will scratch herself until she is raw. Spot-ons and chewable flea preventives are easy to use and highly effective, and should be given regularly to prevent fleas entirely. Some also prevent ticks.

If your dog has fleas, talk to your veterinarian about the best treatment. Bear in mind that your entire home and all other pets in your home will also need to be treated.

Ticks

These are blood-sucking parasites that are most frequently found in areas where sheep or deer are present.

The main danger is their ability to pass a wide variety of very serious diseases—including Lyme disease—to both dogs and humans. The preventive you give your dog for fleas generally works for ticks, but you should discuss the best product to use with your veterinarian.

Ear mites

These parasites live in the outer ear canal. The signs of infestation are a brown, waxy discharge, and your dog will often shake her head and scratch her ear.

If you suspect your dog has ear mites, a visit to the vet will be needed so that medicated ear drops can be prescribed.

How to Remove a Tick

If you spot a tick on your dog, do not try to pluck it off, as you risk leaving the hard mouth parts embedded in his skin. The best way to remove a tick is to use a fine pair of tweezers, or you can buy a tick remover. Grasp the tick head firmly, and then pull the tick straight out from the skin. If you are using a tick remover, check the instructions, as some recommend a twist when pulling. When you have removed the tick, clean the area with mild soap and water.

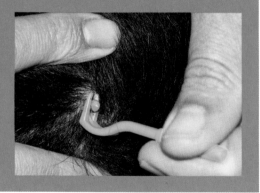

Cheyletiella mange

These small, white mites are visible to the naked eye and are often referred to as "walking dandruff." They cause a scruffy coat and mild itchiness. They are zoonotic—transferable to humans—so prompt treatment with an insecticide prescribed by your veterinarian is essential.

Chiggers

These are picked up from the undergrowth, and can be seen as bright red, yellow, or orange specks on the webbing between the toes, although this can also be found elsewhere on the body, such as on the ear flaps. Treatment is effective with the appropriate insecticide, prescribed by your vet.

Skin mites

There are two types of parasite that burrow into a dog's skin. Demodex canis is transferred from a mother to her pups while feeding. Treatment is with a topical preparation, and sometimes antibiotics are needed. Refer to your vet.

The other skin mite is sarcoptes scabiei, which causes intense itching and hair loss. It is highly contagious, so all dogs in a household will need to be treated, which involves repeated bathing with a medicated shampoo.

Common ailments

As with all living animals, dogs can be affected by a variety of ailments, most of which can be treated effectively after consulting with your vet, who will prescribe appropriate medication and will advise you on how to care for your dog's needs.

Here are some of the more common problems that could affect your Bulldog, with advice on how to deal with them.

Anal glands

These are two small sacs on either side of the anus, which produce a dark brown secretion. The anal glands should empty every time a dog defecates, but if they become blocked or impacted, a dog will experience increasing discomfort. He may lick at his rear end, or scoot his bottom along the ground to relieve the irritation.

Treatment involves a trip to the vet, who will empty the glands manually. It is important to do this without delay or they could become infected.

Dental problems

Good dental hygiene will do much to minimize problems with gum infection and tooth decay. If tartar accumulates to the extent that you cannot remove it by brushing, your dog will need to be anesthetized for a dental cleaning by the veterinarian.

Diarrhea

There are many reasons why a dog has diarrhea, but most commonly it is the result of scavenging, a sudden change of diet, or an adverse reaction to a particular type of food.

If your dog is suffering from diarrhea, the first step is to withhold food for a day. It is important that he does not become dehydrated, so make sure fresh drinking water is available. However, drinking too much can increase the diarrhea, which may be accompanied with vomiting, so limit how much he drinks at any one time.

After allowing the stomach to rest, feed a bland diet, such as white fish or chicken with boiled rice for a few days. In most cases, your dog's motions will return to normal and you can resume normal feeding, although this should be done gradually.

However, if this fails to work and the diarrhea persists for more than a few days, you should consult your vet. Your dog may have an infection, which needs to be treated with antibiotics, or the diarrhea may indicate some other problem that needs expert diagnosis.

Ear infections

The Bulldog has small, rose-shaped ears that fold back, allowing air to circulate. Unlike dogs with drop ears, Bulldogs tend not to get ear infections. However, they still need to be cleaned and checked regularly.

A healthy ear is clean, with no sign of redness or inflammation, and no evidence of a waxy brown discharge or a foul odor. If you see your dog scratching his ear, shaking his head, or holding one ear at an odd angle, you will need to consult your vet. The most likely causes are ear mites, an infection, or there may be a foreign body, such as a grass seed, trapped in the ear.

Depending on the cause, treatment is with medicated ear drops, possibly containing antibiotics. If a foreign body is suspected, the vet will need to carry out further investigations.

Eye problems

The Bulldog has round eyes that should not be too sunken nor too prominent, thus minimizing the risk of injury. However, you need to regularly check your Bulldog's eyes; if they look red and sore, he may be suffering from conjunctivitis. This may or may not be accompanied with a watery or a crusty discharge. Conjunctivitis can be caused by a bacterial or viral infection, it could be the result of an injury, an adverse reaction to pollen, or a congenital defect.

You will need to consult your vet for a diagnosis, but in the case of an infection, treatment with medicated eye drops is effective. Conjunctivitis may also be the first sign of more serious inherited eye problems, which will be discussed later in this chapter.

Foreign bodies

In the home, puppies—and some older dogs—cannot resist chewing anything that looks interesting. This is can apply to the Bulldog who may have a destructive urge, and with his powerful teeth and jaws, he can shred the unshreddable! It is therefore essential that the toys you choose for your dog be suitably robust.

But bear in mind that children's toys may prove irresistible, and some dogs will chew—and swallow—anything. Indigestible items could obstruct your dog's intestine, which is potentially lethal.

The signs to look for are vomiting, and a tucked-up posture. The dog will often be restless and will look as if he is in pain. In this situation, you must get your dog to the vet without delay, as surgery will be needed to remove the obstruction.

Heatstroke

The Bulldog's head, with the short muzzle and flat nose, means he has a tendency to suffer from respiratory problems. He also has a low tolerance for heat and can overheat quickly, resulting in excessive panting and physical distress.

When the temperature rises, make sure your dog always has access to shady areas, and wait for a cooler part of the day before going for a walk. Never leave your dog in the car, as the temperature can rise dramatically—even on a cloudy day. Heatstroke can happen very rapidly, and unless you are able to lower your dog's temperature, it can be fatal. The signs

of heatstroke include heavy panting and difficulty breathing, bright red tongue and mucous membranes, thick saliva, and vomiting. Eventually, the dog becomes progressively unsteady and passes out.

If your dog appears to be suffering from heatstroke, this is a true emergency. Lie him flat and then cool him as quickly as possible by hosing him down or covering him with wet towels. As soon as he has made some recovery, take him to the vet.

Lameness or limping

There are a wide variety of reasons why a dog might go lame, from a simple muscle strain to a fracture, ligament damage, or more complex problems with the joints, including inherited disorders. It takes an expert to make a correct diagnosis, so if you are concerned about your dog, do not delay in seeking help.

As your dog becomes elderly, he may suffer from arthritis, which you will see as general stiffness, particularly when he gets up after resting. It will help if you ensure his bed is in a warm, draft-free location. If your Bulldog gets wet after exercise, be sure to dry him thoroughly.

If your elderly dog seems to be in pain, consult your vet, who will be able to help with pain relief medication and nutritional supplements.

Gastric dilatation/volvulus

This condition, commonly known as bloat or gastric torsion, is occurs when the stomach swells visibly (dilatation) and then rotates (volvulus), so that the exit into the small intestine becomes blocked, preventing food from leaving. This results in stomach pain and a bloated abdomen. It is a severe, life-threatening condition that requires immediate veterinary attention (usually surgery) to decompress and return the stomach to its normal position.

There appears to be several risk factors, and by taking the following precautions, you can reduce the risk.

- Feed two or more smaller meals per day.
- Do not allow the dog to drink a large volume of water at one time.

- Do not feed immediately before or after strenuous exercise—wait at least two hours.

Skin problems

If your dog is scratching or nibbling at his skin, first check he is free from parasites.

In the summer months, your Bulldog might be afflicted by wet eczema, either through a bite or sting, or simply by developing a hot spot and scratching it. What starts as a small, circular abrasion can, within hours, develop into a red, weeping patch the size of a dinner plate if not dealt with immediately.

Make sure you keep a bottle of liquid antiseptic in the medicine cabinet and liberally douse the affected area with a dilution of this if you notice the smallest sign. Your vet will probably prescribe antibiotics and a cream, but if you are able to contain it at the outset, you may avoid an ugly, painful bare patch that takes a considerable time to disappear.

An allergic reaction can also cause major skin problems, but it can be quite an undertaking to find the cause of the allergy. You will need to follow your vet's advice, which often requires eliminating specific ingredients from the diet, as well as looking at environmental factors.

Inherited disorders

The Bulldog does have a few breed-related disorders. If your dog is diagnosed with any of the diseases listed here, it is important to remember that they can affect offspring, so it is not wise to breed affected dogs.

There are now recognized screening tests that enable breeders to check for carrier and affected individuals, and hence reduce the prevalence of these diseases within the breed. DNA testing is also becoming more widely available, and as research into genetic diseases progresses, more DNA tests are being developed.

Brachycephalic airway obstruction

This affects the Bulldog and other brachycephalic breeds because of the way they are constructed. The foreshortened muzzle and flattened nose, combined with an overlong soft palate, can cause difficulty breathing. Signs range from snuffling and snorting, a reduced ability to exercise, and, in severe cases, collapse.

This is most evident in hot and humid weather, so take great care to ensure your Bulldog does not over-exert himself.

Congenital deafness

This appears to be linked to the piebald gene, with deafness resulting from degeneration of the blood supply to the cochlea—a spiral cavity in the inner ear—during the first few weeks of life. There are tests that can assess hearing when a puppy is five weeks of age.

Cryptorchidism

This is a condition in male dogs where one or both testicles fail to descend into the scrotum. The testicle or testicles remain within the inguinal canal or within the abdomen, which can cause complications. Surgery is the best option for affected dogs.

Mitral valve dysplasia

This is a congenital heart defect; a puppy is born with a malformed heart valve between the two chambers of the left side of the heart, which affects its ability to pump blood. This can vary from being very slight to causing heart failure. A detailed ultrasound examination is needed to assess the extent of the problem.

Eye problems

Entropion is a condition in which the eyelid turns inward, scratching the cornea or conjunctiva. If untreated, it can cause permanent damage and blindness. It is extremely painful and is easily detected, because the dog will blink excessively and his eyes will be watery. Surgery is reasonably straightforward and effective. Affected dogs should not be bred.

Keratoconjunctivitis sicca, also known as dry eye, occurs when there is inadequate tear production. The eye becomes dry and itchy; the cornea may become ulcerated and scarred, resulting in loss of vision. Treatment is geared to stimulating the tear glands and administering artificial tears for the rest of the dog's life.

Hip and elbow dysplasia

In dogs with hip dysplasia, the ball and socket joint of the hip develops incorrectly so that the head of the femur (ball) and the acetabulum of the pelvis (socket) do not fit snugly. This causes pain in the joint, and may be seen as lameness in dogs as young as five months old, with deterioration into severe arthritis over time.

Elbow dysplasia is a developmental disease where the elbow does not mature correctly and signs of lameness are usually seen in younger, large-breed dogs. Bulldogs have a high incidence of ED, and so it is essential that all breeding stock is tested.

Gentle exercise, keeping the dog at a good weight, anti-inflammatory drugs, and home management are all part of the treatment for both structural problems. Severe cases may require surgery.

Bulldogs, like many other breeds, can be affected by both hip and elbow dysplasia, and all potential breeding animals should therefore be screened. Hip X-rays are submitted to the Orthopedic Foundation for Animals (OFA) or PennHIP, where they are graded according to the degree of hip laxity. OFA also certifies elbows.

Both disorders are thought to have a genetic component, but the

mode of inheritance has not been established, since multiple genes are involved. Environmental factors, such as nutrition and rapid growth, may also play a role in their development.

Patellar and elbow luxation

This is an orthopedic problem, where the dog's kneecap slips out of place because of anatomical deformities in the joint. Treatment involves rest and anti-inflammatory medications. The characteristic sign is when a Bulldog hops for a few paces and then resumes his normal gait when the patellar goes back to the right position. Surgery may be needed in severe cases but, generally, a Bulldog will live with this condition and be largely unaffected, although arthritis may occur in the stifle in later life. The Orthopedic Foundation for Animals (OFA) grades the degree of luxation or certifies that a dog is clear, based on X-rays.

The elbow joint can also be affected by congenital luxation. The first signs of lameness are seen in the front limbs when a Bulldog is around four to five months of age. Surgery is effective.

Summing up

This has been a long list of health problems, but it was not my intention to scare you. Acquiring some basic knowledge is an asset, as it will allow you to spot signs of trouble at an early stage. Early diagnosis very often leads to the most effective treatment.

The Bulldog as a breed is a generally healthy, energetic dog with a zest for life, and annual check-ups will be all she needs. As a companion, he will bring many happy memories in the years you will spend together.

Find Out More

Books

Bradshaw, John, *Dog Sense: How the New Science of Dog Behavior Can Make You a Better Friend to Your Pet*, Basic Books, 2014.

Eldredge, Debra, DVM, and Kate Eldredge, *Idiot's Guides: Dog Tricks,* Alpha, 2015.

Eldredge, Debra M., DVM, Liisa D. Carlson, DVM, Delbert G. Carlson, DVM, and James M. Giffin, MD, *Dog Owner's Home Veterinary Handbook*, 4th Edition, Howell Book House, 2007.

Stilwell, Victoria, *Train Your Dog Positively: Understand Your Dog and Solve Common Behavior Problems Including Separation Anxiety, Excessive Barking, Aggression, Housetraining, Leash Pulling, and More!*, Ten Speed Press, 2013.

Websites

www.akc.org American Kennel Club

www.bulldoginformation.com The Bulldog Information Library

www.bulldogclubofamerica.org Bulldog Club of America

www.petmd.com PetMD

www.ukcdogs.com United Kennel Club

agility   in this case, a canine sport in which dogs navigate an obstacle course

breed standard   a detailed written description of the ideal type, size, shape, colors, movement, and temperament of a dog breed

conforms   aligns with, agrees with

docked   cut or shortened

dysplasia   a structural problem with the joints, when the bones do not fit properly together

heatstroke   a medical condition in which the body overheats to a dangerous degree

muzzle   (n) the nose and mouth of a dog; (v) to place a restraint on the mouth of a dog

neuter   to make a male dog unable to create puppies

parasites   organisms that live and feed on a host organism

pedigree   the formal record of an animal's descent, usually showing it to be purebred

socialization   the process of introducing a dog to as many different sights, sounds, animals, people and experiences as possible, so he will feel comfortable with them all

spay   to make a female dog unable to create puppies

temperament   the basic nature of an animal, especially as it affects their behavior

Index